Kids At Hope:

Every Child Can Succeed, No Exceptions

*Dispelling the myth that kids are at risk.

John P. Carlos
Co-Author of the International Best Seller
"Empowerment Takes More Than A Minute"

Rick Miller
Founder, Kids At Hope

With Forewords by
Ken Blanchard
Co-Author of the One Minute Manager Book Series

&

Rosey Grier
Chairman, Impact Urban America
and Former NFL Great

Published by

Sagamore Publishing LLC
804 N. Neil St.
Champaign, IL 61820

http://www.sagamorepub.com

Library of Congress Control Number: 2006935260

ISBN-10: 1-57167-531-0
ISBN-13: 978-1-57167-531-6

Printed in the United States of America

Dedication

This book is dedicated to our grandchildren, who are our Kids at Hope.

Madison Oleno

Megan Oleno

Kaitlyn Antunes

Delaney Antunes

Gabrielle Heredia

Jakob Emilio Heredia

With Special Tributes To

Par, Mrs. "J" and Judy, The Johnsons

Of the Lazy J Ranch,
Canoga Park and Malibu, California

AND

Clay Hollopeter

Boys and Girls Club of San Gabriel Valley

Between them, they have created
tens of thousands of Kids at Hope!

Foreword
by Ken Blanchard

When John Carlos asked me to write the foreword for his book *Kids at Hope: Every Child Can Succeed, No Exceptions* co-authored by Rick Miller, I was thrilled for two reasons. First of all, I'm a big fan of John Carlos. The title on his business card sums it up. John calls himself "The Story Teller." He is one of the greatest teachers I know. He has always cared about the plight of kids. In fact, in the 20 years before we became friends, John had already worked with the Foundation for the Junior Blind as a coach for multi-handicapped blind children, for Rancho San Antonio "Boys Town of the West" as a counselor and Saddle Club director and for three different member agencies of the Boys & Girls Clubs of America. So, John is not only a great teacher, he is also one of the most caring human beings I know.

The second reason I am happy to write this foreword, is that I really think *Kids at Hope* could be the most important book written in the last decade to remedy the crisis of despair and lack of hope among our youth in America. I've known for a long time that the mind and the computer are similar in one way. They don't readily know the difference between the truth and what they are told.

If you put information in a computer, it doesn't ask, "Where did you get those figures? Those figures are wrong!" The computer does whatever it can with what you give it. For a long time, we've described the computer's ability to process information as "garbage in, garbage out." The same is true of the mind. The mind does not know the difference between the truth and what you tell it. If you get up in the morning, look in the mirror and say, "You are fabulous," your mind doesn't say, "Who are you kidding? I know better."

So, how we program kids' minds and what we put in is really important. I think John and Rick are really onto something. For a long time, we've talked about kids "at risk." What a self-fulfilling prophecy that is—whereas *Kids at Hope* is all about every child having the capacity to succeed, no exceptions.

Now, positive thinking isn't the only thing that's great about this book. I learned by working with Norman Vincent Peale on our book, *The Power of Ethical Management,* that when people read his classic book, *The Power of Positive Thinking,* sometimes they assumed all you had to have is positive thinking. Norman said, "That's not true. You also have to take some action. Just thinking positively isn't going to make you succeed." What do you *do* to succeed?

What's great about *Kids at Hope* are the tremendous ideas in here about what can be done in schools and communities to really create a culture of hope.

It's important that you hear the word "culture" because this book is not about establishing programs. Programs come and go, but if you can create a *culture* of hope, then everything that's done is done to help every kid succeed.

The big thing that Carlos and Miller emphasize is that everyone in our schools and the community, in the home and everywhere, should be responsible for kids' successes. These authors have great suggestions. In fact, they talk about the four aces that kids should have in their hands.

- Kids need anchor parents—parents who absolutely love them unconditionally and are there to support them.

- Kids need other caring adults (heroic figures)!

- Kids need high expectations and supportive adults who encourage kids to reach for goals that may, to the child, seem unattainable but are actually within reach.

- Kids also need opportunities to succeed.

So, read this book. Use this book! I believe it's the answer to empowering our kids to become the successful, happy adults they deserve to become.

Now, let me turn this foreword over to my friend and colleague, Rosey Grier. Rosey is a National Football League great, having played with the New York Giants, but he is best known as one of the Fearsome Foursome of the Los Angeles Rams. He has worked with the youth in this country relentlessly for over 30 years.

Recently, Rosey and I appeared before a U. S. Congressional committee that was looking into the drug situation in this country. Before we had a chance to speak, the senior congressman on the panel said, "I want to put it on the record that I am honored to be in the presence of Rosey Grier. A lot of people come and go around popular movements and ideas, but when that goes down, they're gone." He said, "Mr. Grier, you have devoted your life to supporting and encouraging and helping the youth, and I value that."

That's who Rosey Grier is. That's how much he cares about what John Carlos and Rick Miller are writing about.

Foreword
by Rosey Grier

I love *Kids at Hope*. I think this is a fabulous book. When I first started traveling around the country into urban areas to help the youth, I was appalled by the run-down buildings I saw. In becoming familiar with those environments, I realized the buildings and apartments where people lived were not only run-down, but they were symptomatic of the lack of vision and hopelessness of the people. I concluded that when people change, the entire environment changes. Helping people change has been my quest for more than three decades. I want to make a difference for these young people, and so do John Carlos and Rick Miller.

One of the reasons I am excited about *Kids at Hope* is that not only are John and Rick trying to show people how to change kids' attitudes, but they are working on developing kids' skills and talents. This will enable kids to possess the tools necessary to make their lives more meaningful. When a person is prepared, and the opportunity presents itself, she or he is able to seize that opportunity and be productive.

Education is the molding force in preparing youth for their future endeavors. Creative teachers establish the atmosphere that is conducive for learning. Kids are motivated when the right atmosphere for learning is present. Singer BMX explains in a rap, "First, I'm going to crawl, then I'm going to walk, then I'm going to stand, then I'm going to talk, then I got to learn, then I'm gonna' teach, then I'm going to burn and I'm gonna reach." It's up to everyone involved in the lives of children to encourage kids to continue reaching.

Great attitudes and great skills will bring great success to everyone. Read *Kids at Hope.*

It is a continual challenge to set the stage for learning. Get your school and community involved in this important challenge to bring out the best we can in the young people of this country.

Table of Contents

Chapter One: The Visit 23
Everyone has a different task at school but we all have the same job, and that is, to ensure the success of all our children, no exceptions.

Chapter Two: The Classroom 33
We help our children succeed holistically.

Chapter Three: What Makes a Difference?   45
You must first reach a child before you can teach a child.

Chapter Four: No Exceptions! 51
For children to win the game of life, they need aces. Adults have the aces and must deal them to the children. The more aces we deal children, the greater their chances of success.

Chapter Five: Defining Success 65
The more success opportunities you offer children, the more successful children you will have. Defining smart: What the world needs and what you have.

Introduction

Since its original publication in 2001, *Kids at Hope* has truly captured the hopeful imagination of tens of thousands of caring adults across the country. Their belief in the potential of every young person has been restored and revalidated by this book. Each year over 3,000 "treasure hunters" from many walks of life are introduced to the Kids at Hope belief system and strategy through one of our professional development seminars, institutes, classes, train the trainer events, books, videos, or keynote addresses.

Over the past several years, as we have established Kids at Hope models in communities, youth organizations, recreation sites, fire and police departments, and schools we have a much better understanding of the popular adage, "It takes a village to raise and educate a child." We know that statement is true, but it begs two questions: Who trains the village and who in the village is invited to the training? Once you can articulate the question it makes it much easier to find the answer. We have learned that the capacity of Kids at Hope offers a model of training that reaches out to every adult, not because of their educational or professional status, but simply and most powerfully because of their interest in our youth.

As you will discover through the adventures of our story protagonist, Robert Dawson, identifying the elements, which support a child's success or adds to their failure requires an open mind and a willingness to see a future, which doesn't exist. That has always, and will always be the only way we can shape our future. So, our basic question is, can we see a future where all children can succeed and there will not be any exceptions? It hasn't been easy changing the paradigm and associated culture, which has taught us that many children are at risk and therefore we shouldn't expect much from them. As a matter of fact, one state in our union, planners look at second grade achievement scores as part of the formula they will need to determine how many prison cells they will require in the future. Talk about a self-fulfilling prophecy. I cannot imagine giving up on children in the second grade. I cannot imagine ever giving up on our kids. That is exactly what we do everyday without even knowing it. The youth at risk label has prematurely judged our young people guilty until proven innocent. An entire industry has been created by the at risk label. We have responded to the guilty verdict and the at risk culture by ordering our youth to enter a series of prevention programs. For every pathology or potential pathology, we have created a separate program or activity to help children avoid negative and damaging behavior. Although laudable at first glance, these prevention programs have institutionalized the at risk stereotype to the point where we have ignored our children's assets and strengths in order to focus on their problems and deficits. By doing so we have unconsciously prohibited many children from achieving their unique scholastic, spiritual, social, and emotional resources and related multiple intelligences.

Yet, in the face of these odds, Kids at Hope continues to make remarkable progress. I guess we are proving the renowned anthropologist Margaret Mead correct when she said, "Never doubt that a small group of thoughtful, committed citizens can change the world; indeed it's the only thing that ever has." I have come to respect and appreciate Dr. Mead's expression in action, and not just words. I wish I could say Kids at Hope had the uncompromising enthusiasm and leadership of many. We did not. What we did have was the commitment and shared vision of a few. And that was enough.

On behalf of all the children who have benefited from our efforts and who without question would have wallowed in the purgatory known as at risk programs, I thank each and every one of you—you know who you are. I also thank those individual and groups who are sharing their imagination in providing the intellectual, emotional, and financial capital needs to advance Kids at Hope.

While I am quite excited with this newly revised edition of our book, *Kids at Hope: Every Child Can Succeed, No Exceptions* I am saddened that my co-author and dear friend John Carlos' sudden death in 2004 is not with me to share this important achievement. John's spirit, however, is alive and strong in this book and the phenomenal message and action it offers in support of the success of all children, no exceptions!

Rick Miller
Founder and Chief Treasure Hunter
Kids at Hope

Background

In the early 1980's, the National Commission on Excellence in Education presented a study entitled "A Nation at Risk." It's findings concluded that kids were considered to be "at risk" only to do something bad. We classified these "at risk" children as latch-key kids, kids from single-parent homes, kids with too much free time on their hands, kids who lacked structured after-school activities, and kids who were potential gang members. Yet, no one realized what the effect might be on the kids who were told they were "at risk." Did it occur to anyone that once a child hears that he or she is "at risk" to do something bad, chances are, they'll believe it? And chances are, if they believe it, they'll eventually "be it."

This notion implied that kids could not be trusted to be "at hope." In other words, it is wrong to assume that all kids want to be successful in life.

Or so they told us. Well, we personally had a hard time believing that kids woke up in the morning, looked in the mirror, and said to themselves, "Today, I will fail!"

"Supervise them closely, keep them busy and always be on guard," we were told. "A place to go and a way to grow," was the mantra of the typical recreation program of the 1970s and 1980s.

Many of these programs seemed to work to a degree and, in and of themselves, there was nothing wrong with keeping kids occupied with positive stuff. Yet, we just didn't think it built the citizens of tomorrow, but rather placated the kids for the short term. Most of these after-school programs did not go far enough in addressing developmental needs beyond "keeping 'em busy." To be fair, we did not think schools did enough to build character either. We thought, "There should be programs that say a child has worth, makes a difference, and can succeed." We thought, "There should be programs that score beyond scholastic and athletic achievement. Programs that give credit for eagerness, humor, serving, caring, sharing, problem solving, and the ability to get along with others, in effect, an emotional report card."

It turns out we were both right, and wrong. Right about the need to change people's thinking, and wrong about the need for more programs. It became clear that we first had to attack the belief systems.

How do we create a society where people with different talents can succeed? It's simple. The systems have to change both in the corporate world and in the world of family and education. It takes more than a village to raise a child; it takes a culture!

A culture can be created. A culture simply needs a common belief system reinforced by programs and the everyday behaviors of adults as they interact with children on a daily basis. The adults must provide this positive interaction 24 hours a day—whenever dealing with kids.

I recall a study that said kids want three things:

- **Children want to know they make a difference in the world.**

- **Children want to have a circle of friends they can trust.**

- **Children want an anchor adult or heroic figure in their lives.**

In an article published in September 1997 by the *Journal of the American Medical Association,* Michael Resnick, Ph.D., Peter Berman, Ph.D., and Robert Blum, M.D., examined many aspects of school environments to determine why some kids have healthier behaviors and better physical health than others. They discovered that only one specific aspect of school life—a feeling of connectedness to school-was responsible for better health and healthier behaviors among the students.

According to James Garbriano, Ph.D., a world renown psychologist and professor at Cornell University, a number of characteristics and conditions are directly related to a young person's capacity to be resilient and succeed in life:

- **A stable positive relationship with at least one person, someone absolutely committed to the child and to whom the child feels a strong, positive attachment. Children need to feel loved!**

- **Authentic self-esteem. This is more than just feeling good about oneself. It is the ability to maintain a psychological reservoir to deal with life's ups and downs.**

- **Social support from persons and institutions outside the family. Children need to feel connected and to experience pro-social behavior that serves to reinforce the core values of the community and society.**

Dr. Garbriano says that the resiliency and success of children in attaining these characteristics are dependent upon children having adult "anchors" in their lives in terms of:

- **Spiritual Anchors, to deal with the deeper meaning of life.**

- **Psychological Anchors, who support a child's ability to deal with life's ups and downs.**

- **Social Anchors, who can help counteract and serve as counterweight to any socially toxic behaviors demonstrated by family, schools, and community- which are often present in our lives.**

We agree. We believe that children want to know that they make a difference in the world, that children want to leave a circle of friends who they can trust, and that children want an anchor adult or heroic figure in their lives. This book is about those anchor adults and how they affect our children's successes. *Let's begin!*

One

The Visit

"WELCOME to Harrison, a Kids at Hope City, where the local time is 6:55 a.m.," came the announcement over the airplane's speakers.

"A Kids at Hope City?" questioned Robert Dawson silently. "Is that what the flight attendant said?"

Robert gathered his personal belongings and as he approached the plane's door he stopped for a moment to speak to the flight attendant.

"Did you say something about a Kids at Hope City?" queried Robert.

"Yes sir," the polite attendant responded, "Harrison is a Kids at Hope City."

"What is a Kids at Hope City?" asked Robert.

"Simply speaking it's a community. . .," the flight attendant was interrupted by a gate agent who apparently had an emergency. "Sorry, got to go," the attendant apologized and quickly disappeared into the jet way.

Robert's interest was peaked, but he had an appointment he needed to rush to so off he went to claim his baggage. As he boarded the down escalator he noticed an illuminated display advertising a sign. "Welcome to Harrison, A Kids at Hope City." At the bottom of the sign appeared the city logo which read "Incorporated 1946." On the other side of the sign was a sunburst logo which read "Kids at Hope No Exceptions!"

Interesting was Robert's immediate thought. He believed this intriguing secret would soon be revealed.

After picking up his checked bags and rental car, Robert headed off to his 9:00 a.m. appointment with Mildred Ramirez, principal of Lincoln Elementary School.

Robert stopped for a moment. It was 8:00 a.m. and traffic was unusually lighter than he had expected. He arrived for his appointment much earlier than scheduled. The extra 30 minutes was a welcomed luxury. Robert normally ran late for his meetings. But not this time. Robert had a moment to catch his breath before his customary busy day. He seemed to truly enjoy the fact that life had slowed down, and instead of feeling like a hostage of time, he began to observe the rhythm of students, teachers, and staff preparing for another school day. He headed toward the school office.

"Sometimes you miss a lot of important things when you are so busy being busy," he thought.

"Stop and smell the roses," he remembered his wife telling him. And for a moment, he was "smelling the roses."

A school bus stopped and Robert watched as the students disembarked. Curiously, the bus driver caught Robert's eye.

As each child left the bus, the driver was overheard encouraging the children. "Do your best today. I'm proud of you," he said to every boy and girl, looking each one directly in the eye. A few students actually stopped and whispered something in the driver's ear. This was exchanged for a smile and off the children ran to their classrooms.

Robert was surprised by the interaction just witnessed. After the bus was unloaded, he approached the driver.

"Hi, and excuse me," Robert said, as he extended his hand to the driver. "My name is Robert Dawson and I'm visiting from the U.S. Department of Education."

"Hello, my kids call me 'chief,'" responded the bus driver, as he shook Robert's hand.

"I couldn't help but notice how you interacted with each of the students on your bus," Robert offered. "I mean, you seemed to genuinely express interest in each and every one of them."

"Well, they're my kids," Chief proudly noted. "I know what you are thinking. Bus drivers drive buses, teachers teach, and administrators administer."

"I guess that is what I'm getting at," Robert said.

"Not here," Chief said. "At our school, we are all responsible for our kids."

"Could you please explain what you mean by that?" Robert asked.

"Sure. When I applied for this job, I filled out a regular application. You know, name, address, and experience, the whole ball of wax. But when I was interviewed, everything was…how would you say, 'a bit unusual'?"

"I'm not quite following you," Robert said.

"Well, in my previous bus driving jobs, I am normally interviewed by the director of transportation or a high-level supervisor. The questions are usually the same. But this interview was anything but normal. First, the committee was made up of the principal, a teacher, parents, and transportation supervisor. They all interviewed me. They asked me questions about how driving a bus could help a student succeed in school. I confess that question floored me. Why would they be asking me that type of question? After all, I wasn't applying as a 'teacher.' I just wanted to be a bus driver. It's not rocket science, you know?" Chief said.

Robert asked, "What happened?"

"Well, the interview committee said, 'All our employees must focus on the end result...the success of all our kids'," Chief answered.

"Do you know what my title is?" Chief asked Robert.

"School bus driver I assume," Robert responded.

"You're half right," Chief said. "It's bus driver and treasure hunter."

"Sorry to cut this short but I have a field trip I need to prepare for," noted Chief. "Nice meeting you."

"Same here," said Robert.

As Chief boarded his bus and drove off, Robert glanced at the back of the bus where that same Kids at Hope logo appeared. **NO EXCEPTIONS** it boldly read.

"May I help you?" asked a friendly voice from behind the school counter.

"Hello, I'm Robert Dawson and I have a 9 a.m. appointment with Mrs. Ramirez."

"Welcome to Lincoln Elementary a Kids at Hope School," offered the Secretary.

"Hmmm," Robert thought out loud. "A Kids at Hope School, a Kids at Hope City, a Kids at Hope bus. Hmmm."

The Secretary just smiled at Robert as he contemplated his thoughts.

"Please be seated, Mr. Dawson. I'll let Mrs. Ramirez

know that you are here," the school secretary said.

Robert sat and waited. He enjoyed the extra time. As Robert waited, two students, a boy and a girl, ran up to the counter.

"You're late for class," the secretary noted.

"We woke up late and missed the bus. Mom had to drive us," the boy confessed.

"Wait here and I'll get you a pass to get you into your classes. Don't make this a habit, OK?" the secretary added.

"OK," the children agreed.

The secretary returned with the late passes.

"Now, quickly, before I give you these passes, tell me about something in which you succeeded in yesterday," the secretary requested.

Robert, listening to the conversation, found the question odd. However, the girl, whom he believed to be eight years old, blurted out, "I won the spelling bee!"

"Good for you, Leah," complimented the secretary. "How about you Torry?" she asked.

"I don't know," was Torry's response.

"What do you mean you don't know? In our school everyone succeeds everyday, somehow and somewhere," the secretary encouraged.

"Not Torry," his sister piped in. "He got a bad grade on his writing exercise yesterday."

"I'm sure he'll do better next time. Right, Torry?" asked the secretary. "Although grades are very important, they are not the *only* way to measure success. Can't you think of something you did well yesterday, Torry?" the secretary persisted.

"I helped my mom with the dishes and she said I did a good job," Torry recalled.

"That's good! That's good!" responded the secretary. "There are lots of ways to succeed in life and they are all important. Good job, Torry and good job, Leah. I'm proud of the two of you. Now get to class, pronto!"

A few seconds after the children ran out of the office, Mildred Ramirez, the school principal greeted Robert.

"I'm sorry I made you wait, Mr. Dawson. Welcome to our Kids at Hope school," Mrs. Ramirez said.

"It's no problem. I've really enjoyed watching your staff interact with the students," he said.

"Would you like something to drink, Mr. Dawson?" Mrs. Ramirez asked.

"A cup of coffee would work," Robert said.

"Coming up," responded Mrs. Ramirez. "So, what brings you all the way from Washington, D.C.?" she asked.

"I'm preparing a report for the Secretary of Education about exemplary school programs and your school was recommended for observation," Robert answered.

"I'm flattered, Mr. Dawson. What would you like to know?" Mrs. Ramirez asked.

Before addressing his formal questions, Robert was anxious to know about what he had seen earlier.

"When our plane landed this morning the flight attendant welcomed us to Harrison, 'A Kids at Hope City,'" stated Dawson. "There was a sign at the airport also welcoming us to a Kids at Hope City. I saw the Kids at Hope logo on one of your buses and both you and your secretary refer to Lincoln Elementary as a Kids at Hope school. So what's the story behind the story?" asked Robert.

"Well, let me try to explain," offered Mrs. Ramirez.

"About seven years ago, this school was having a lot of problems. Performance was low, behavioral problems were high, morale was low, and teacher turnover was high. We needed to take some action—and fast—or we were headed for real disaster."

"What did you do?" Robert asked.

Treasure Hunter: a caring adult who searches beneath the surface to find all the talents, skills, characteristics, and intelligence which may be buried in our children or youth, and can be easily overlooked, but when discovered, enriches our world.

"We realized that the job of educating our children was not just the responsibility of the school and its teachers, but that the entire community had a role in the success of our children. Our quality of life is directly tied to their successes. So, we not only redefined all our roles in terms of the end result. For example, 'success' rather than 'job descriptions'," Mrs. Ramirez responded. "We engaged our entire city in a remarkable experiment."

"Why don't I give you a tour? It's easier to understand if you see it in action," Mrs. Ramirez said.

WE ALL HAVE DIFFERENT TASKS BUT WE SHARE THE SAME JOB AND THAT IS, TO HELP CHILDREN SUCCEED.

Dawson's Reflection:

There was a "Chief" in my life. It was in the third grade but he was not a bus driver. He was the school janitor, but neither I nor any of my classmates ever thought of him as the janitor. He was "Ed." Ed always had kind words. I can still hear his Irish brogue saying "Top 'o the mornin' to everyone." I remember him sharing his lunch and his time with us. He always offered to help us clean up our mess at the lunch table. He had this old army jeep. We thought it was so cool. I wonder now if Ed wasn't really a teacher in disguise.

Everyone is a teacher, huh? Why does that make me think of my vacation in Ireland? Ah, yes, the boomerang. I remember now. It was a supermarket, SuperQuinn.

When we entered the market, the first thing my wife said was, "How strange. The employee name tags are shaped like miniature boomerangs."

I thought, "Boomerangs don't belong in Ireland. They belong in Australia."

I approached the man at the meat counter and asked, "What's with the boomerang?"

The man smiled and replied, "Well, what does a boomerang do when you throw it?"

I answered, "It comes back."

He said, "That's our job, to make you want to come back. Our jobs aren't just cutting meat, stocking bags, operating the till, or doing maintenance. Those are our individual tasks, but our job is the same. And that is, to make sure you come back. Cutting meat is just a task, something I do. What I am accountable for is the experi-ence you have in our store. What can I do to make you want to come back?"

Interesting, why didn't I see these connections before?

Two

The Classroom

MRS. RAMIREZ and Robert entered Mrs. Alicia Rashad's fifth-grade classroom as quietly as possible to avoid disturbing the students. Within a split second, however, all the heads in the class turned to look at the two visitors.

"Please excuse the interruption," Mrs. Ramirez said.

"Welcome," returned Mrs. Rashad.

"This is our guest, Mr. Dawson," Mrs. Ramirez told Mrs. Rashad and the class. "He is visiting from the United States Department of Education."

A murmur spread through the classroom. The students looked at Robert and determined that he was a very important person.

"Please continue," urged Mrs. Ramirez. "We will be extremely quiet."

"Martha, will you please lead the class in the Pledge of Allegiance?" Mrs. Rashad asked.

The class joined Martha in the recitation of the Pledge.

"And Thomas, will you please lead the class in the Kids at Hope Pledge?" asked Mrs. Rashad.

"Kids at Hope Pledge?" Robert wondered.

The class joined Thomas in reciting the following, "I am a Kid at Hope. I am talented, smart and capable of success. I have dreams for the future and I will climb to reach my goals and dreams every day."

"Never heard that one before," Robert thought.

No sooner did he fully understand that which he had just heard, when his eyes began to dart from student to student. Something was different, but he couldn't quite place it. Then it became clear. Every student was wearing a T-shirt signifying a college or university.

Mrs. Ramirez was watching Robert carefully, trying to read his expressions as he was introduced to a series of new concepts.

"Pretty interesting," he thought. Mrs. Ramirez read Robert's thoughts.

All eyes returned to Mrs. Rashad after the brief interruption.

"What's today?" she asked.

"Report card day," cheered the class.

"You are correct," Mrs. Rashad said.

Each student seemed excited to receive a report card and the children were completely focused on the stack of cards Mrs. Rashad was holding in her hand.

She called each student's name, and one by one the children eagerly approached Mrs. Rashad and collected their report cards. When they returned to their desks, they anxiously opened their cards and read what their teacher had written. Each student giggled at the results.

"Funny," Robert thought. He had witnessed this custom for many, many years. He remembered his own experience as a young student. It was a day of celebration for some, disappointment for others and *as expected* for everyone else. But within this classroom, it seemed like a big celebration.

After allowing the students time to absorb the information she had given, Mrs. Rashad asked the class to quiet down.

"I'm so proud of each of you," Mrs. Rashad said. "I am so very proud of you," she repeated.

The students giggled and applauded. Most importantly they were happy with their achievements.

"Report Card Day," Robert thought, "seems more like the last day of school."

"Time to go," Mrs. Ramirez said.

"Ah, OK, sure," Robert acknowledged.

Mrs. Ramirez and Robert walked into an empty hallway. Classes were in session and the corridor was quiet.

"So, did you see or hear anything interesting?" Mrs. Ramirez asked.

"Yes, quite interesting," Robert replied.

"Well?" questioned Mrs. Ramirez.

"Well, when we first walked in and the students recited the Pledge of Allegiance, I assumed it was the start of a typical school day. But then the oath caught me completely off guard," Robert noted.

"What was that oath called again?" Robert asked.

"That's our Kids at Hope Pledge," answered Mrs. Ramirez.

"Kids at Hope Pledge?" Robert repeated. "What does it all mean?"

"It's a simple affirmation to support our belief system that every child can succeed, no exceptions!" offered Mrs. Ramirez. "If we believe it about our students, they need to believe it as well. They need to be able to say the words, hear the words and most importantly understand and practice the words."

"I know what you are thinking," offered Mrs.

Ramirez.

"You do?" asked Robert.

"Yes, you think the oath may be too simple and possibly trite," continued Mrs. Ramirez.

"Well, it did cross my mind," responded a surprised Robert.

"Well, it is simple but it is also enormously powerful," answered Mrs. Ramirez. "But don't underestimate the simple but powerful message that it offers which becomes part of our overall culture."

"Why 'Kids at Hope'?" Robert asked.

"Because it is the opposite of that which we have believed and accepted much too long and that is: our children are *at risk*. They aren't *at risk* and we have popularized that expression to the detriment of recognizing the hope which lies in all our children!" offered Mrs. Ramirez. "Our students and all children are in fact at hope."

"We will learn more about that later," concluded Mrs. Ramirez. "Was there anything else that you noticed?" she asked.

"The kids were all in college T-shirts or sweatshirts," observed Robert.

"Yes, the T-shirts," acknowledged Mrs. Ramirez, "are also part of our belief system. Education is a life-long experience and that is an important message to our youth. We want all our students to know, in no uncertain terms, that we believe in them and we wish to encourage them to pursue higher education. Keeping the high-bar high is important, and in doing so, we create a culture which supports that belief. Having children wear college-emblazoned shirts, at least once a quarter is a simple way of reinforcing that belief. Sometimes our teachers invite our alumni to talk about their college experiences. We want our children to see these former students as role models. We want them to understand that college is an attainable goal for everyone. In fact, one of the homework assignments we give our older students is to prepare a paper on the college of their choice, usually reflected by the T-shirts they wear, and to present their findings to the class. We want them to know what happens in a university and what makes the college they have chosen so unique."

"I've never thought about it before, but I hear what you are saying. If you believe that all your children are capable of success, you will treat them that way," offered Robert. "I remember that my brother and sister-in-law dressed their newborn in a baby T-shirt representing the college they attended. I guess they were already establishing a belief that my nephew would go to college."

"It was an early expectation," Robert added.

"That's right," reinforced Mrs. Ramirez. "We realize that children who go to college have that goal instilled in them at an early age. It's no different from the expectation or assumption that every person needs a job. It's something you do when you grow up. We, therefore, create a culture which supports our belief that all children can succeed. There is another thing we do at our school which supports our belief system."

"What is that?" Robert inquired.

"All our students know their respective graduation dates," Mrs. Ramirez said.

"High school graduation?" Robert asked.

"No, all our children know their college graduation dates," Mrs. Ramirez informed her surprised guest.

"Every one?" Robert asked.

"Every one," answered a proud Mrs. Ramirez. "First-graders through our eighth-graders all know and have always known what date they will be graduating from college. Remember, our culture is about high expectations and *NO EXCEPTIONS!*"

"Reminding our students about our high expectations for them shows that we believe them capable of achieving that goal. Having caring adults support that expectation and creating the opportunities to ensure such achievement, is what we should always be about," she continued.

"We're also not naïve. Every child may not choose go to college, but they all know they have that option and they can succeed," Mrs. Ramirez concluded.

"That all makes great sense," a pleased Robert stated. "I must also confess that I wasn't sure what the report card scene I witnessed was all about."

"Yes, the report card scene. Very interesting don't you think?" asked Mrs. Ramirez. Mrs. Ramirez spoke to Mr. Dawson about her concern as well as those shared by many of her parents. Too much emphasis being placed on grades, which only measures behavior and little, if any, importance on potential. At Lincoln School everyone knew the importance being placed on grades but it didn't exclude their respect and recognition that the years in school and out of school programs must include a focus on potential.

Mr. Dawson liked the concept, but like so many others determined that there was not any way one could measure potential. Mrs. Ramirez again emphasized the value of treasure hunting.

"You see," offered Mrs. Ramirez, "treasure hunting is all about looking beyond the behavior to identify the potential in children. Treasure hunters use the Kids at Hope report card as one of the tools needed to go beyond test scores and grades. Observations and judgment about conduct and behavior ensure every child understands that they possess great talent, skills, characteristics, and traits. If we can identify those attributes, expose, and develop them, great positive results will be achieved, academically, emotionally, and socially. It is incumbent on adults to do so."

"Our Kids at Hope report card," continued Mrs. Ramirez," which recognizes that although reading, writing and math are critically important in life, you need additional skills, talents, and intelligence to succeed. It's a report card which recognizes that success is not just a score or a grade in a subject matter. It's about what we call *total* success."

"Total success?" Robert asked.

"You see, Mr. Dawson, the reason for education is to help children succeed in life. But first you must define success. If we can't define success, then all we are doing in school is offering a set of classes, subjects, and programs without clearly and dramatically defining their value to the elusive term we call success," explained Mrs. Ramirez.

"So, how do you define success?" Robert asked.

"Totally, holistically. In other words, we realize that success isn't some *thing,* but rather a series of destinations on the road of life. It isn't just a grade, or job, or money, but it is a journey. The journey includes success in home and family, success in education and career, success in community and service and in hobbies and recreation."

"This is where life's journey is going to take you. So you see, life is about succeeding at all four destinations," Mrs. Ramirez went on.

"Therefore, the important question is: what are the skills, talents, characteristics, and intelligence needed to succeed at each of life's destination points." The report card is about those talents, skills, characteristics, and intelligence required for success in life. In other words, these report cards underscore what we have said about our children early in their life, but which we have forgotten later on. That is, we believe each child that comes into the world is unlike any other person. Their uniqueness is their strength and that allows them to make a difference in the world. Why steal that from them?" she asked.

"So, our report cards honor their uniqueness and offers them insight as to how those talents can be helpful in the real world. For example, is kindness and creativity of equal value with reading and math? The reality is, it is! Therefore, the reason our students get excited about this report card is that it celebrates their unique contributions to the world. It's about our beliefs and how we support our belief in our children," she explained.

"That cannot happen in a program but must exist 24

hours a day, seven days a week, in all we do and say," stated Mrs. Ramirez.

"So what you are saying, is that there are lots of ways to be smart?" Robert offered.

"Yes, indeed," answered Mrs. Ramirez. "How do you define 'smart,' Mr. Dawson?" continued Mrs. Ramirez.

"That's a good question," replied Robert.

"Yes, I know," offered Mrs. Ramirez. "Try this as a definition: 'Smart is what the world needs and what you have.'"

"Very interesting," Robert responded. "What the world needs, huh? Well?

Well, the world needs good doctors but it also needs honest people. And the world needs engineers but it also needs compassionate people. Is that the gist?"

"Yes, Sir," replied Mrs. Ramirez. "And that can only happen if we as adults understand that although we have different tasks, we all share the same responsibility and that is, that we are all treasure hunters. Our superintendent is a treasure hunter. Our bus drivers are treasure hunters. Our police officers are treasure hunters and our parents are treasure hunters," she said. "In other words, every adult must be a treasure hunter. Keep in mind that along with our culture of *NO EXCEPTIONS* also includes high academic standards for all our students. However, we don't teach to the test we teach to the students. By doing so, our students then reach personal excellence."

"What is your title again, Mr. Dawson?" Mrs. Ramirez asked Robert.

"Director of Programs," he replied. "Oh and a treasure hunter, I guess," Robert said.

"That is absolutely correct," Mrs. Ramirez said happily. "A culture that values children doesn't just define its role in terms of tasks—which appear on a business card— but also in terms of a job—which is what we represent to children as adults. A culture in which adults accept their primary responsibility as treasure hunters, and will provide a caring society. One that will be effective with its youth," she explained.

Dawson's Reflection:

This reminds me of a seminar I attended years ago called "Succeeding at Your Moment of Truth." Jan Carlzon, president of Scandinavian Airlines (SAS) shared his company's customer service philosophy. He called it "Moments of Truth."

From the moment a passenger decides to fly SAS until he reaches his destination, he comes in contact with five SAS employees. Each employee must "win" when it's his turn with the customer.

"What good does it do if four employees 'wow' the customer and the fifth employee alienates him?" Carlzon asked. "The customer will remember the employee who was rude or discourteous, thus making the whole flight a miserable experience."

This "destination point" approach to helping children is the same. A child has to win at each destination point. All of us— parents, family, teachers, coaches, club leaders, religious leaders, and even everyday citizens—

have a responsibility to make sure kids have opportunities to be successful. We need to consciously ask ourselves, "What am I doing to make a difference in a child's life?"

I see how important it is to make sure that each contact a child experiences at school is a successful contact. If a student has contact with a bus driver, cafeteria helper, janitor, principal, vice-principal, nurse, and six teachers there are a lot of opportunities for failed "Moments of Truth."

What if, as Mrs. Ramirez suggests, the task is not the job? What if the real job is to give children experiences that will help them be successful?

Three
What Makes a Difference

ROBERT and Mrs. Ramirez retreated to the faculty lounge for refreshment.

"You seem a little haggard, Mr. Dawson," observed the principal.

"I guess I am," Robert responded. "Here are my questions."

Robert questioned Mrs. Ramirez for the next 45 minutes about her school's history, its dramatic turnaround, and its exemplary programs. Mrs. Ramirez was patient in her responses and took her time to fully answer his questions. But Mrs. Ramirez did not talk much about programs. She talked about her culture.

"Whether we know it or not, all schools, organizations, and communities have a culture. That culture can work for you, or it can work against you," offered Mrs. Ramirez.

"When our school was failing, which meant our students were failing, it was rooted in our culture, and it wasn't just in our school, it was throughout our community."

"The expectation from our history was that our students don't do well. They are not achievers so they are not expected to achieve. And without thinking about it, we lived up to those expectations. It became a selffulfilling prophecy. We were on automatic pilot, going through the motions and not understanding how our culture was controlling us," Mrs. Ramirez explained.

"No program, no curriculum, no computer, no pay raise on the face of the earth is going to change a culture that is aimed at failure. We needed to change our culture and to do that, we needed to understand what our community truly believed in," she said.

"Believed in?" asked Robert. "What does that have to do with teaching our children?"

"Everything," answered Mrs. Ramirez.

"You see, we didn't know what we believed in. We knew our mission was to teach our children. But did we, as individuals, truly believe that was possible? Many believed that if we just found the right program or the right curriculum, children would succeed. We were looking for the magic potion. There was no easy answer, but there was a *simple* answer. We did some serious soul searching. We asked every one of our staff— and that means everyone—to write out a personal mission statement as it related to children. We did that because we wanted to know if the people responsible for 'teaching' our children truly believed that our children would succeed. If they did not, then they did not belong on our campus."

"It wasn't that they were bad people, it was that their personal mission statements were not in sync with our mission, our belief that all our children are capable of success and that there are no exceptions. That belief must operate 24 hours a day, seven days a week, 365 days a year. It was a basic, yet powerful belief that everyone needed to share our chances in realizing that mission wouldn't end up as empty words on a plaque in our halls," she said.

"Am I making sense, Mr. Dawson?" asked Mrs. Ramirez

"Please continue," Robert replied.

"It is hard at first not to reduce our success to the mechanics of a program. It's imperative that this success begins with a belief system. Our culture is no more than acting out our beliefs," explained Mrs. Ramirez. "It is the sum total of our actions."

She went on, describing that the success of the school drew its breath, its magic, and its life from each person on the campus.

"I hate to say it, but many of our staff didn't believe all our children could succeed. Some employees were emotionally retired on the job and some were exhausted from fighting battles they felt they could not win. Again, they weren't *bad* people, but their belief system did not support our mission," stated Mrs. Ramirez. "I hate to admit it, but we had lots of students who similarly believed that they were incapable of success."

"I see," Robert responded.

"Did you have good teachers, Mr. Dawson?" Mrs. Ramirez asked.

"Yes, I did," he replied.

"Did you have bad teachers?" Mrs. Ramirez continued.

"Yes."

"What was the difference," asked Mrs. Ramirez, "between the good teachers and the bad?"

"Well, let's see," answered Robert. "The good teachers seemed to believe in me. They never gave up on me. They were always there for me. They had positive energy and high expectations of me."

"And the bad teachers?" Mrs. Ramirez asked.

"They seemed to go through the mechanics of teaching, but couldn't relate to the students," Robert said.

"That's right, Mr. Dawson!" she responded.

"When we think about our own experiences and how they helped us succeed, we remember the people who believed in us. I have yet to hear any of our former students say that they were really grateful to a particular teacher for teaching them to do long division, phonics or algebra. The students remember the teacher who believed in them, who supported them, who helped them succeed, not just in a subject matter, but in life," Mrs. Ramirez said.

"Your point, Mrs. Ramirez?" Robert asked.

"The point, Mr. Dawson is that to *teach* a child, you must first *reach* a child!" exclaimed Mrs. Ramirez.

The point is, that to teach a child, you must first reach a child.

Dawson's Reflection:

Have we forgotten those experiments in education from so long ago... The Pygmalion experiments I think they were called. The name was taken from the George Bernard Shaw Play "Pygmalion," later turned into a movie called "My Fair Lady." In the movie, Eliza Dolittle said the only difference between a lady and a flower girl from the docks is the way you treat them. If you treat me like a flower girl from the docks, I'll behave like that. If you treat me like a lady, I'll behave like a lady. In the movie, she was accepted as the princess of the ball because she was treated that way. In the education experiments, if you thought a student was dumb, you tended to treat them like they were dumb. My freshman year of high school they had four home rooms, 9A, 9B, 9C and 9D. 9A and 9B were the college prep classes and C and D were the lesser classes. Boy, talk about a subliminal message. Of course every child may not win, that's not the point, the adults in their lives must act as if they could, is the POINT. Years ago, I talked to a boy in juvenile detention and asked him what his parents would say about him ending up here. His answer still haunts me. "They'd be very proud, all my life they told me I was going to end up in jail!" How often do we do that as parents? Say things like thief, liar, brat, spoiled, etc... instead of dealing with behavior, we label the child?

Four
No Exceptions!

"OOPS, it's almost 11 o'clock. Time flies when you're having fun, right Mr. Dawson?" asked Mrs. Ramirez.

"Right, Mrs. Ramirez," Robert responded.

"We have a meeting with our No Exceptions Team leader," Mrs. Ramirez said.

"No Exceptions Team?" Robert asked.

"Come along. I think you will find this meeting interesting," teased Mrs. Ramirez.

"From what I have seen so far, I have no doubt about that fact," Robert replied.

Mrs. Ramirez and Mr. Dawson strolled over to Jim Smith's classroom. This was Mr. Smith's lunch hour and he scheduled a meeting with the principal to discuss his team's efforts.

"I took the liberty and had the cafeteria make us up a few sandwiches," Mr. Smith said as his guests arrived.

"Thank you, Jim. This is Mr. Dawson," introduced Mrs. Ramirez.

"Yes, we knew you would be visiting today. So far so good?" asked Mr. Smith.

"To say the least," Robert said.

"Mrs. Ramirez asked if I would take a few moments and talk about our No Exceptions Team," Mr. Smith said.

"Please, I am anxious to hear about your program," encouraged Robert.

"Oh no, Mr. Dawson. This isn't a program. It's part of our culture," responded Mr. Smith.

"Sorry, I should know that by now. Old habits are tough to break," Robert apologized. "I came here to learn about your exemplary programs and I have yet to see one. I think I'm beginning to understand the culture concept, but I have to admit I am still a little confused."

"Don't worry. We all were when we started," confessed Mr. Smith. "I was probably the worst of the naysayers on our faculty. When I heard that we were going to change our culture, I said, 'Here we go again, the new flavor-of-the-month syndrome.' I was wondering, 'How long will this flavor last?' I was also concerned about the time and effort that would be required. You know teachers...we are not short on 'things to do.' Anything extra creates the impression that this could be the straw that breaks the camel's back."

"So what did you do?" asked Robert.

"Not much at first," offered Mr. Smith. "I approached this concept with the attitude that I would go through the motions, but my heart wouldn't be in it."

"What changed your mind?" Robert asked.

"Mrs. Ramirez scheduled an in-service training which I wasn't too keen about. But then everything began to change. It wasn't the typical in-service training of just more stuff," related Mr. Smith

"I'm not following you," Robert said.

"The training was focused on each and every one of us. It challenged us to look at ourselves, our successes. It challenged us to define success. It challenged us to recognize whether we were first, honest to ourselves, and what that means to our children. And it wasn't preachy. As a matter of fact, it was fun to recall the many people that helped us to succeed. We learned a concept called Success Links," continued Mr. Smith. "What we learned during the workshop was that there are a common set of experiences or links, which had the power to help children succeed. And those links are within each of us and yet, over the years we tend to forget what they are."

"Well, what are they?" asked Robert.

"Too easy just to tell you. If I did, it would just be information. So let me just ask you about your own success," Mr. Smith offered.

"OK. I'll play. What do you want to know?" Robert asked.

Mr. Smith said, "I want you to think of a giant anchor chain in the form of an 'S'. This stretch of chain would require about 50 links."

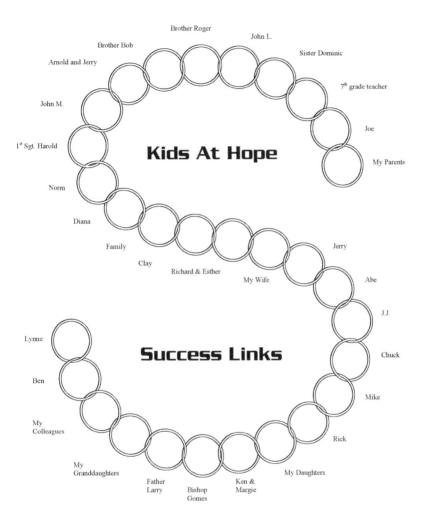

Litany of the Links
The Success Links Chain of Robert Dawson

- My parents: for always having faith in me and for being there for me,
- Joe: our crossing guard who called me 'Einstein,'
- My seventh grade teacher: who always believed I could master problems that seemed too difficult,
- Sister Dominic: who befriended my family and always encouraged me,
- John: my best friend in grade school, for accepting me,
- Brother Roger: my high school counselor for four years,
- Brother Bob: who saw me through 60 hours of detention and kept me in the game,
- Arnold & Jerry: my friends and employers,
- John: my best friend for a number of years, who taught me loyalty,
- 1st Sgt. Harold: he taught me the real skills of leadership,
- Norm: who taught me dedication and commitment,
- Diana: a co-worker and girlfriend, who taught me compassion,
- My brothers and my sisters-in-law: who taught me about FAMILY,
- Brother John: who taught me that everyone has something to offer the world,
- Clay: who taught me tenacity and allowed me to volunteer at his youth organization,

- Richard and Esther: life-long best friends, who taught me loyalty and compassion,
- My wife: who continues to teach me unconditional love,
- Jerry: my first boss who taught me the importance of training people,
- Abe: a friend and board member of my Boys' Club, who taught me about volunteerism and dedication,
- J.J. and John: my board presidents, who taught me what true volunteers are,
- Chuck: who hired me to run his camp and taught me acceptance,
- Mike: who taught me so much about philosophy and creativity,
- Rick: who hired and promoted me and who taught me to see beyond!
- My daughters: who taught and continue to teach me Joy,
- Ken and Margie: who continue to teach me friendship, acceptance and Spirit,
- Bishop Gomes: who reminded me of the importance of Faith and friendship,
- Father Larry: my pastor, who continues to teach me the power of values,
- My granddaughters: who have re-taught me the meaning of unconditional love,
- My colleagues: for sharing and unconditional acceptance——always!
- Ben: who has always supported me,
- Lynne: who loves me no matter what.

"For an anchor chain to do its job, it must be strong. Now, think of each of those links as a Success Link, that is, a positive experience or person in your life that, in effect, strengthened your chain of development," Mr. Smith added.

"I just want you to think about those outside events or people who encouraged and supported you. In other words, what influenced your success?" Mr. Smith asked.

"You mean, like good teachers?" asked Robert.

"Yes, like good teachers, but also everything or everyone else you can think of that helped you to achieve your success thus far," suggested Mr. Smith.

"Well, I would have to say my parents were my first success, my first link," Robert stated.

"Think of a six-foot-wide sign inside that first link on a football field with your parents' names on it," interrupted Mr. Smith. "Other thoughts?" Mr. Smith continued.

"Teachers, some coaches, a close friend of the family and boy, I haven't thought about this person in a hundred years, but a man named Joe," Robert recalled.

"What did Joe do for you?" asked Mr. Smith.

"He smiled at me every day as I walked to school. He called me 'Einstein,' made me laugh," answered Robert.

"Who was he?" asked Mr. Smith.

"The crossing guard," Robert replied with a smile.

"Anyone else or anything else that supported your success?" continued Mr. Smith.

"Let's see, my seventh-grade math teacher always believed I could master problems that seemed too difficult," recalled Robert. "I was never a good math student, but my math teacher believed in me—not just about math—but he seemed to just believe in me. He told me I could do anything I put my mind to...That's about it. Wait, I seem to recall that I learned that I was good at many things. I was good at sports, I was good in school, and I had a lot of friends. I think being good at things in your childhood helps you to succeed in adulthood," Robert said.

Mr. Smith interrupted, "Don't forget your Success Links. All those people and things you named must be reflected in a link."

Robert was reflecting on his answers. He was enjoying his brief journey back to those early years.

"Well, that's it!" interrupted Mr. Smith.

"That's what?" asked Robert.

"That's it!" exclaimed Mr. Smith. "I'm not trying to be cute or smart but what you described is 'it.' You see, what you remember about growing up is true for most people. Simply put, *we* learned from our own experiences and the experiences of others, that if you offer children a set of Success Links, you can remarkably improve their chances to succeed. And how do we know? Because it worked for us and people like us."

"We understand that all people need food, water and oxygen. We understand that all people need shelter and a sense of security. We need to also understand that all people, especially children, need a common set of Success Links and experiences, which dramatically improve their opportunities to succeed. All people need a set of these links to support their successes," Mr. Smith said.

"And what might those links be?" inquired Robert.

"Just what you said," responded Mr. Smith. "To help

ensure a child's success, having an anchor parent is critical. Other caring adults are also critically important, and we believe, the more the merrier. The more people who care about a child, the greater the chance of that child succeeding. We also know that children need someone who not only sets high expectations for them, but who also believes in them sometimes more than they believe in themselves. And finally, we learned that success breeds success. One strong link builds on another strong link. But we must also acknowledge that failure breeds failure. That's why we do not focus on negative links. We must help children develop a pattern of success, not by ignoring failure, but by focusing on success. We must, as people did for us during our childhood, create opportunities which showcase all a child's talents, skills, characteristics, and intelligence. In effect, we must become a Success Link in the lives of children."

I'm not talking about self-esteem. That comes next. Self-esteem is the end result of successes. All too often, we limit the number of ways we allow children to succeed," Mr. Smith explained.

"We need to redefine success in terms of real life skills, recognizing that success requires many talents, characteristics, and intelligence, which often times go unrecognized," Mr. Smith added.

"Wow, you covered a lot of ground, Jim," Robert said.

"It's still fairly simple. Mrs. Ramirez tells us to think about a card game in which you deal cards to each player. In life, the best cards we can deal our children to help them win the game of life are four aces."

Those aces are represented by:

- **An anchor/parent:** someone responsible for a child's emotional and physical well being 24 hours a day, seven days a week, in an unconditionally loving way.
- **Other caring adults:** "The more the merrier," the more adults a child can perceive as caring about him, the greater his chance for success.
- **High expectations:** represented by someone who believes in you more than you believe in yourself, who believes you can achieve things you may not believe you are capable of achieving. These are our Treasure Hunters.
- **Opportunities to succeed:** Create a pattern of success. Acknowledge that failure breeds failure.
  (See four aces envelope in front of book)

"What happens if children get only three of the aces, or two of the aces, or just one of the aces?" Robert asked. "What happens if some children don't get any of the aces? Does that mean that they are doomed to fail?"

"No, Sir. It just means we have to help them be better players. And it's easy to do so," Mr. Smith replied.

"It is?" asked Robert.

"Yes, because as you know, as adults we have the aces in our hand," answered Mr. Smith. "Parents could be better parents. Teachers, youth leaders, friends, family, and others can be the other "caring adult ace," and the "high expectations ace" and the "opportunities to succeed ace." In other words, we as adults hold many of the aces in our hand and it is our job to make sure we deal them to children who are missing those aces. It's as simple and as powerful as that."

"So what does that have to do with your No Exceptions Team?" interjected Robert.

"My team's job," stated Mr. Smith, "is to work with the entire school and reach out to our community to ensure that our children leave our school with aces in their hands, no exceptions!"

"That sounds fine and dandy, but how do you ensure that children are in fact receiving aces? It sounds good in theory, but to be candid it seems more wishful thinking than practical," offered a suspicious Robert Dawson.

"It does, doesn't it? That's what I thought too," replied Mr. Smith. "When I first heard about the importance of aces, I could not fathom how we could guarantee that all our children receive aces until Mrs. Ramirez introduced our aces chart."

"Aces chart?" repeated and questioned Mr. Dawson.

"Yes, aces chart," continued Mr. Smith. You see unless we have an objective measurement that all our children are receiving aces we in fact our fooling ourselves and once again failing our children."

"So, what did you do?" pursued Robert Dawson.

"We put up a chart with all our students names on it in our faculty and staff lounge. We then invite all the people who work or volunteer at the school to visit the chart every three months and if they have a meaningful relationship with one or more of the students, defined by one of the four aces, they mark their name next to the students," explained Mr. Smith. "If we see a student with limited aces or no aces we know that student is disconnected and enrolled in our school anonymously. It raises a red flag and now we can do something about it."

Robert Dawson was pleased again to learn the schools understanding of the importance of significant relationships was translated into action with results.

Dawson's Reflection:

I traveled here to view a once struggling school that is now singled-out for its success. I heard about this school's innovative programs. I came to see those programs firsthand. After four hours, I have yet to see anything close to what I expected. But something is happening here, something special.

The school's turnaround seems to be based on a mission statement change, supported by a cultural change. And everything else that happens is in support of the mission and culture. Furthermore, the mission isn't just the school's mission, it is the personal mission of each and every person the school employs—from principal to bus driver, to cafeteria worker, to teacher, to custodian, and on and on. More importantly, the mission is spread through the school's culture, not through programs, but through the interpersonal relationships between adult and child.

My concern is that a culture is not as easily "canned" for public consumption as a curriculum is. We can put together manual materials; video and other support materials, mail them out and have schools adopt the elements. But, how do you "can" a culture? How do you package a successful culture and replicate it? Seems like that may ultimately be the $64,000 question for Mrs. Ramirez and her staff.

Five

Defining Success

"MR. DAWSON, we are holding a call for you in the office," announced the school secretary over the intercom.

"Go ahead and use my office," offered Mrs. Ramirez. "I'll join you in a second."

"Hello, Dawson here!"

"Hi, Bob. This is Deborah. Sorry to disturb you, but I wanted you to know that the Secretary has called a big meeting for early Friday and it's important that you be there."

"I'll be there," Robert replied. "Thanks for the call."

"Is everything OK?" asked Mrs. Ramirez.

"Oh, yes. The Secretary of Education has called an important meeting for Friday and all hands must be on deck," Robert explained.

"Are you ready to continue our tour, Mr. Dawson?" Mrs. Ramirez inquired.

"In a moment. But I do have one question. Something's bothering me," Robert replied.

"What is it?" Mrs. Ramirez asked.

"As you know, I came here to learn to about your program, but I have come to understand the remarkable culture and the belief system that you have created," he replied. "I am concerned that, although laudable and obviously effective, it may be difficult to package. What are your feelings?"

"'Too early to answer that, Mr. Dawson. There are

still some major elements that you need to witness before I am able to answer that question," Mrs. Ramirez responded.

"All right. I'm putting my trust in your good hands," Robert sighed.

"Come on then. It's time for you to meet our Passport to the Future Advisory Committee," Mrs. Ramirez said.

"Passport where?" asked Robert.

"To the future. Come along," encouraged Mrs. Ramirez.

Mrs. Ramirez and Robert walked to the library. Waiting for them in a conference room were eight people who had just gathered and were chatting informally.

As Mr. Dawson and Mrs. Ramirez entered, a man walked up to Robert and extended a hand.

"Hello, I'm Bill Modeleski, chairman of the Passport to the Future Advisory Committee."

"Robert Dawson, U.S. Department of Education."

"Good to have you here. Time to get started. Hello, Mrs. Ramirez," Mr. Modeleski said.

"Hi, Bill. Go ahead. Mr. Dawson and I will sit over here," Mrs. Ramirez said.

Mr. Modeleski asked everyone to be seated and formally welcomed Robert to the meeting.

The committee members then introduced themselves. The committee included: two parents, Donald and Isabella Kelly; a pediatrician, Janet Osgood; the president of the neighborhood association, Michael Roasto; a local community college professor, Harold Byers; school police resource officer, Don Pope; fire fighter, Dan Lewis; a representative from the city parks and recreation department, Leo Schultz; chair of the No Exceptions Team, Carl Evans; school custodian, Bob Anders; a representative of the local chamber of commerce, Karen Burns; and the executive director of a nondenominational faith-based ecumenical council, Paul Eppler.

"Looks like everyone made it today," observed Mr. Modeleski. "Mr. Evans, will you fill us in on the Passport to the Future Fair your committee has been planning?"

"Everything is on track," reported Mr. Evans. "We are planning on using the playing field this year instead of the field house. We have a sub-committee chair for each of life's destination points: Home and Family, Education and Career, Community and Service and Hobbies and Recreation. Our theme this year is 'The Successful Journey.'"

"Each student will receive an actual 'Passport to the Future' and each destination page will have at least five blanks for stamps that the students must earn to successfully pass through that destination point. The stamps will be placed on the passport according to the destination point that is being visited."

"Could you give us an example of how a student earns a stamp?" Mr. Modeleski asked.

"Sure," answered Mr. Evans. "We have invited fellow treasure hunters from all over the community. We divide them into each destination point. A group is assigned Home and Family, another Education and Career, and so on. The students then visit each destination point and 'interview' our guests. They try to determine what talents, skills, traits, characteristics, and intelligence each treasure hunter needed to succeed at their destination point. The goal is to identify as many different skills, talents, etcetera needed to succeed at each of life's destination points."

"In other words, we are reinforcing the concept that success is what happens on the journey to life's destination points," continued Mr. Evans. "We wish to also reinforce that success in life requires many talents and skills including reading, writing, math, and science as well as honesty, integrity, sense of humor, unselfishness, and the such. Accordingly, to show struggle in life, the children discuss roadblocks that could interfere with those positive characteristics that are stamped on their Passports," Mr. Evans said.

"In fact," Mrs. Ramirez interjected, "at the end of the fair, these group sessions called Challenge Reviews, allow students and adults to discuss the characteristics listed on their Passports. They must identify the challenges that life will present to their strengths and then discuss the challenges they have in coping with any obstacles."

Mrs. Ramirez signaled to Robert to join her outside the library's conference room.

"As you already recognized, Mr. Dawson, our programs and activities are enhancements to our mission and culture. However, the last major element has to deal with what it is that we are supposed to do in school," Mrs. Ramirez said.

"Supposed to do in school?" Robert asked.

"It seems that every year or so, a new initiative is passed by the school board or state legislature or department of education," Mrs. Ramirez explained. "Each has a new or different idea as to what is supposed to happen within the four walls of our school. Some people believe we are just about academics. Some think constant testing is the answer. Others believe we are here to teach values. Some groups require character education. Others feel the school must also be a social service agency. We have many expectations put upon us and each one seems to be disconnected from the other. Our priorities seem to shift, thus further confusing our staff."

"So, what did you do about it?" asked Robert.

"We realized that the success of our efforts and those of the home and the balance of society are dependent on each other," answered Mrs. Ramirez. "After stripping away all the politics, all the self-serving interests and all the confusion, we concluded that all our jobs are the same: to help children succeed in life. But to begin, we must define success. After many meetings, we concluded that success is what happens on the journey to life's destinations," she said.

"That was a powerful conclusion because it gave meaning to life, not just to a set of skills but the recognition of the talents, skills and intelligence that are required to succeed at each of life's four major destination points," she said.

"That's amazing, Mrs. Ramirez," declared Robert.

"We think so too," agreed Mrs. Ramirez.

"The fact that you identified life's four major destination points captures a framework that makes all that we do with children less fragmented and more holistic," Robert offered. "Furthermore, the fact that the four destination points are all-encompassing and engages a community to support the success factors needed in life. And the fact that life needs so many talents to succeed creates more of an opportunity to succeed rather than less. All too often we have unwittingly created more opportunities for one to fail than to succeed. You have reversed that."

"That's an important observation," noted Mrs. Ramirez. "For example, when I was growing up in a little community, we were offered four sports in which to chose from if we wished to participate in athletics. Those sports were football, basketball, baseball, and track and field. The emphasis was on boys. And even the boys who were not fond of or good at those sports found themselves on the sidelines."

"I'm not sure I'm following you, Mrs. Ramirez," Robert said.

"Well, if you only offer four sports that are for a select group of boys, then you limit the number of opportunities for all children to succeed athletically," responded Mrs. Ramirez.

"Today, if you return to that community, you will see dozens of sports offered and the end result is that you will see more boys and girls succeeding athletically," Mrs. Ramirez explained.

"Are you suggesting that we often limit the opportunity for our children to succeed?" Robert asked.

"Not only am I suggesting it, I am saying it is a fact of life," replied Mrs. Ramirez. "In too many schools, we tell our students that success is limited to reading, writing, math, and science. Then we grade them to let them know, again unwittingly, that some of them are better than others. I see this the same way I witnessed the four-sport limitation in my small community. As soon as we created more sports in which children could succeed, the more children we found succeeding. The reality is, that although reading, writing, math, and science are critical, there are other intelligences that are equal to those and we should equally acknowledge and reinforce those intelligences as well. There is no 'upside' to limiting the ways children can succeed."

Mrs. Ramirez shared some insights she gleamed during the Kids at Hope community trainings. "During one of our training activities we ask each adult participant in the room to share their earliest thoughts as to what they wanted to be when they grew up. Without exception every participant listed a job, profession or occupation. They covered the gamete from doctor, lawyer, professional athlete, veterinarian, fire fighter, police officer, movie star, and so forth."

"What's so odd about that?" questioned Mr. Dawson.

"At first nothing until it dawned on me that isn't it a bit strange that everyone replied to the open ended question 'what was the first thing you thought of becoming when you grew up' by responding just with a job, profession, or occupation?"

"Huh?" was all that Mr. Dawson could offer which was reinforced by the blank look in his eyes.

"It was odd because we had understood and accepted that success in life is about contributing to life's four major destinations: Home and Family; Education and Career; Community and Service; and Hobbies and Recreation. Yet, we have become so programmed during our upbringings to limit our thoughts about the future to just a job, profession or occupation when we know our roles and contributions in life must extend well beyond that single dimension," continued Mrs. Ramirez.

"I was so taken by that observation," continued Mrs. Ramirez, "that I asked the teachers if they would ask the same question of their students."

"What happened?" quizzed Robert.

Mrs. Ramirez noted that the answers were just as dramatic. "But to be honest," she continued, "not surprising at all. Our students related their sense of future to just a job, profession, or occupation. Our children need to understand that their futures are not just about a job even though that is important. But equally important is their understanding that the future includes family, community and hobbies and recreation. Life is multidimensional."

"Absolutely," agreed Mr. Dawson, "As adults we realize that life is more than just a job and the happiest of people in our nation are those who have found success and achievement in all aspects of their life not just in one."

"You are correct, Sir!" quipped Mrs. Ramirez. "So you can see we need to continue to explore and develop our children's talents and skills beyond just the ability to get a job but the capacity to contribute to the many opportunities which will be a part of their futures."

"Your insights underscore the importance of ensuring we develop our young peoples emotional and moral intelligences," shared Mr. Dawson.

"Absolutely, and also Howard Gardner's *Multiple Intelligence*," answered Mrs. Ramirez. "How important is it to society to have honest people? Or caring people? Or unselfish people?" she asked.

"Wow, it all sounds great," Robert responded.

"Hold on a second, Mr. Dawson. We have come along way, but we don't pretend we have answered all the mysteries of the universe," Mrs. Ramirez replied with a mildly scolding tone.

"Oh, I know that, Mrs. Ramirez. But my excitement is focused more on what you have accomplished rather than what you haven't. You've created a simple, yet powerful framework, which not only rallies your school, but your entire community to be a part of that journey."

"Now you are getting it, Mr. Dawson," Mrs. Ramirez replied.

"I am. I am," Robert thought. "Success is what happens on the journey, and the more success opportunities you offer children, the more successful children you will have."

Success is what happens on the journey, and the more success opportunities you offer children, the more successful children you will have.

Dawson' Reflection:

I always believed that my goal was to "arrive" at my destination. In truth, the journey was more important than the destination. The career position I have is more the result of my experiences than my promotions! All the ups and downs, all the wins and disappointments, all the pain and sorrow, prove I am the composite of my experiences.

More importantly, these experiences, including the skills, the talents and the intelligence I have acquired, have real-world value. As I arrive at each destination point, including home and family; education and career; community and service; and hobbies and recreation, I'm better equipped to continue my success.

Six
A New Day

THE alarm startled Robert. Morning arrived. He hit the snooze delay button on his alarm, but did not go back to sleep.

It took Robert a few moments to fully awaken. He rubbed his eyes and stretched. "Time to tackle the world again," he thought.

He glanced over at his schedule for the day. His first appointment was with Mrs. Ramirez and Dennis Tinseth. Mr. Tinseth was a high school principal. Mrs. Ramirez's young students would attend Mr. Tinseth's high school.

Mrs. Ramirez met Robert at his hotel at 7:30 a.m. Together, they had an 8:00 a.m. appointment with Mr. Tinseth.

"How far is the high school?" asked Robert.

"We aren't going to the high school. We are headed to the community youth center, which is just across the street from the high school," offered Mrs. Ramirez.

"Are we still meeting with Mr. Tinseth?" Robert inquired.

"Yes we are, but Veronica Jones, director of the community center, will join us," noted Mrs. Ramirez.

Robert thought this schedule change was strange since his primary interest was to explore how education had enabled Mrs. Ramirez to make progress in her school. He considered the visit with a high school principal a bonus. Mrs. Ramirez insisted Robert visit not only her campus but also experience her culture—which claims that every child can succeed, no exceptions. And to experience Mrs. Ramirez's culture, Robert would have to see how this culture exists—outside the four walls of an institution, as well as inside.

Robert was beginning to understand the power of that belief system and culture, but his paradigm blinders only shifted enough to include the high school (another educational institution), instead of seeing how the whole community was involved.

Robert and Mrs. Ramirez entered the community youth center. Veronica Jones was outside admiring the center's new sign. Garfield Community Youth Center was in bold letters with a smaller, yet visible graphic appearing below: Kids at Hope Believed and Practiced Here.

"What do you think, Mrs. Ramirez?" asked Veronica Jones.

"Pretty neat. Looks great," responded Mrs. Ramirez.

"Did you notice the new paint job?" Veronica asked.

"I did," Mrs. Ramirez replied. "We even have Kids at Hope logo decals on all of our buses."

Robert was absorbed in this conversation, wondering what all the excitement was about.

"This is Robert Dawson," Mrs. Ramirez said and introduced the two men.

"Nice to meet you," offered Veronica.

"Same here," Robert said.

A moment later, Mr. Tinseth arrived.

"Great sign, Johnny," announced Mr. Tinseth.

"Thanks. Has yours gone up yet?" Johnny Jones asked.

"Not yet. We are scheduled for next week. They still need to put up the library and park signs," reported Mr. Tinseth.

"Hello, Dennis," interrupted Mrs. Ramirez, addressing Mr. Tinseth.

"Hi, Mildred," Mr. Tinseth answered.

"Meet Robert Dawson," added Mrs. Ramirez.

The men shook hands and exchanged pleasantries. "The more we export our cultural belief through our cultural counterparts, specifically the people in our community, the greater chance we have to realize the belief," stated Mrs. Ramirez. "As I said earlier, we have to demonstrate our beliefs in everything that we do. That is remarkably different from our old habits. Those old habits encouraged us to do our own things in our own way. Youth centers did their own thing, parks and libraries did their thing, the high school did their thing, and so on and so forth."

"To demonstrate to our public as well as to ourselves, we had to find creative ways to express the belief in deeds, as well as anything else we can think of," continued Mrs. Ramirez.

"Well, one thing we came up with is that each of us are physically separated from one another. We take much pride in our individuality, which is great, but we must also take great pride in our shared vision. And part of our vision is that we must suspend self-interest in accomplishing a greater good than any one of us can do alone," explained Mrs. Ramirez.

"Therefore, we wanted to express our shared vision as visually as we could. We wanted to make an architectural or artistic statement that we share a common goal and that is: to help all children succeed. In order to do this, we each agree to give up a little of our individual identity for a greater good. What we decided to do is what you are now witnessing," she continued. "You see, we are all erecting new signs on our individual buildings to link our shared belief system."

"The fact that we don't view children to be 'at risk,' but rather 'at hope,' is a unifying statement which does not require us to give up our unique missions. In fact, this strengthens our overall shared culture," Mrs. Ramirez said.

"Now our citizens can drive by the high school, the elementary school, the community youth center, park, library, and other organizations and recognize that we share a common belief. We are linked not only through signage, but through spirit and effectiveness to do whatever is necessary to ensure the success of all our children. Even our police cars bear a Kids at Hope Community sticker," she said. "The police are a highly visible presence in our community. They are easily recognizable. They offer many services to children and youth beyond law enforcement. They understand the importance of having children succeed. Recruiting the police department to join in this culture underscores the importance of our efforts."

"As our mayor recently said on television when she unveiled the newly-decorated Kids at Hope police cars, something important is happening in our city," Mrs. Ramirez said.

"So what you are saying, is that each organization or

institution that buys into the belief system, will share it publicly with a common graphic and lettering?" Robert asked.

"Not only that, Mr. Dawson, businesses will also connect because we are all here ultimately for the same reason, and that is to pass the torch of leadership and success from one generation to another," Mrs. Ramirez continued. The stickers and signs reflect that 'aces' are given out here and shows that these people, these organizations know how to treat kids."

"Fascinating," Robert thought. "A whole community linked together."

"You see, Mr. Dawson, if we only showed you our school without the rest of the components, you'll only be able to explain how our culture works on campus. The bigger picture may be lost. Kids don't grow up in institutions or agencies. They grow up in cultures. What we are trying to establish is a belief system and structure that supports the success of all our kids. In other words, as a child proceeds through the community, every community member will consider him a young person 'at hope.' Everyone will acknowledge a responsibility to help this child succeed. Remember your earlier question, 'Can this be replicated?'" asked Mrs. Ramirez. "The answer is, 'It depends!' It depends on whether or not the community can agree on the fact that all children are capable of success, *NO EXCEPTIONS!"*

"'Looks like you are really thinking outside the box,'" Robert responded.

"That's an interesting observation," answered Mrs. Ramirez. "I used to think that I was capable of thinking 'outside the box'."

"I think most managers and executives pride themselves on that ability. Unfortunately, only part of that is true. We were able to think outside the box as it related to our own internal mission, goals, and objectives. However, we were not able to think outside our four walls," Mrs. Ramirez explained.

"There is quite a difference between thinking outside the box and outside your walls! That's a bigger challenge, but one necessary to achieve if we are to truly succeed with our children," she said.

"You mean not only do we need to think outside the box to help all children succeed, but we need to be able to think outside our four walls as well?" Robert asked.

"Exactly," answered Mrs. Ramirez. "Follow that up with thinking outside our city, county and state boundaries, until our entire country can see all its children as 'at hope'."

"I'm afraid to ask, but what's next?" inquired Robert.

"Funny you asked," answered Mr. Tinseth.

Mrs. Ramirez described her community's efforts in working with the city government to officially designate an area as Hope Square.

"I know it may sound a little silly, but we are very serious about that description symbolized by the word 'hope.' We are designating the library as our north boundary, the high school as our south boundary, the community center as our west boundary and the elementary school as our east boundary."

"That represents a square mile. Included in this perimeter are about 3,000 people. Accordingly, there are parks, businesses and other groups, which we believe will help identify with this area," Mr. Tinseth explained.

"If you can have Times Square, and Broadway in New York, which identify the theater district; Copper Square in Phoenix, which identifies the downtown; and Fisherman's Wharf in San Francisco, why can't we have Hope Square to effectively describe a number of agencies, institutions, and businesses that share a common identity which we call a belief system?" asked Mrs. Ramirez.

"By going to all this effort, we remind ourselves everyday that we are interconnected and interdependent. We note that the children we serve are not just one organization's children; they are all of our children. It also provides a sense of permanency. Buildings have a way of suggesting continuity because they are always there. Programs don't offer that same sense. That is why we felt it important to express our belief system through our buildings as well as our programs," added Mr. Tinseth.

Robert was impressed by the commitment he was witnessing.

The group was soon joined by the library director and parks and recreation superintendent. The manager of a nearby fast-food restaurant also stopped by. In just moments, many important people who played a number of different roles in the success of children, were all outside the Garfield Community Youth Center admiring the new sign and graphics.

"Very impressive, very impressive," Robert repeated in private reflection.

"Any thoughts?" asked Mrs. Ramirez.

"A community that cares about its children must express such caring in everything and anything they do," concluded Robert.

"You got it, Mr. Dawson," replied Mrs. Ramirez.

A community that cares about its children must express such caring in everything and anything it does.

Seven

The Next Surprise

"WHERE are we off to now?" asked Robert

"It's a surprise," offered Mrs. Ramirez.

"I think you've done a pretty good job surprising me already," Robert joked.

"We are still missing a crucial element on this journey," offered Mrs. Ramirez.

"Aha! The high school! I was hoping we would get around to visiting the high school," Robert said.

"Right! The reason for doing what we do: and that is, to help every child succeed, no exceptions!" exclaimed Mrs. Ramirez. "This couldn't happen if our students didn't themselves believe in what we are doing. Accordingly, it wouldn't work if the students weren't completely involved."

Mrs. Ramirez drove Robert over to the local high school.

As the two walked onto campus, a student greeted them.

"Hello, Mrs. Ramirez. My name is David. We are waiting for you by the picnic tables."

David escorted the two to the picnic table where six students waited.

Mrs. Ramirez asked the students to explain their roles in the belief system of success.

Sarah began by explaining that she heard about a meeting where a belief system was to be explained and that students were being recruited to help. "I wasn't sure what they were looking for, but I was curious enough to attend," Sarah said.

"What I learned was what I felt deep inside already. I learned, however, that it was important that such a belief must be shared with everybody, all the time," Sarah commented.

"And in your words, Sarah, what was that belief?" asked Robert.

"The belief was that every kid is capable of success, no exceptions," answered Sarah.

"What could you do to support that statement, Sarah?" Robert asked.

"Let me answer that question," interrupted Daniel, a senior at the high school.

"Sure, go ahead," Sarah agreed.

Daniel continued, "More than anyone, at this age, kids have a great influence over other kids. We can support our friend's dreams, encourage their hopes, or do the opposite. Too many kids think it's cool to step on other people's dreams. There is, however, a lot more of us who understand that to be a friend, you must support your friend's dreams. We understand that it takes a lot of support to succeed in life and kids can help other kids succeed."

"How do you do that?" Robert inquired.

"My turn," offered Lynne.

"Go for it," encouraged Daniel.

"Simple," continued Lynne. "We share our dreams openly and honestly. We share our strengths. We ask about our perceived weaknesses and what we can do to strengthen them. We work to remain optimistic and we find the best way to do that is to have people around us who encourage us, care about us, and support us. In return, it is our responsibility to do the same for them."

"That's right," Candace jumped in. "High school is tough enough. The last thing we need is a campus that is a 'downer.' That's not to say we don't have our down times. It just means that we make an earnest attempt at keeping the hope alive on campus. Each student, faculty member, administrator, cafeteria worker, school resource officer, everyone is part of the effort. We don't let anyone off the hook."

"How did this all begin?" Robert asked.

"About two years ago, when we were arriving on campus for the start of another school day, we were greeted at the front of the campus by all the teachers, principal, assistant principals, and staff," David said. "They were holding signs which stated that they believed in us. They were cheering us, throwing confetti at us, and handing out balloons. It seemed silly, but I have to confess, it lifted our spirits. We couldn't help but smile at the teachers."

"That greeting was the beginning of our new culture on campus. Everyone began to pull together. Now that I look back on that day two years ago, I realize that something special was happening on our campus," David continued.

"Our school was prepared to do whatever was necessary to ensure the success of its students. I got excited about that. What we didn't realize, was that this was also the beginning of our entire community coming together under the same belief system," David said.

The discussion with the students continued with great spirit for another hour. Robert nearly forgot about catching his flight.

"Thank you, everybody," Robert responded. "You just put a giant explanation point on a truly remarkable two days. I wish you all well and I can't wait to come back and spend more time with all of you."

Robert's final thought as the plane lifted off the ground was, if the future is all about our kids, then everything we do must relate to the future of our kids.

Dawson's Reflection:

Whoa, this goes way beyond "Moments of Truth" and boomerangs! This idea of total involvement is really what drives the culture of Kids at Hope. No one is exempt. We all have a role to play in our community in the development of our kids.

I remember speaking to a cast member at Disney World who told me that everyone is important to the success of the theme park because we all have a role in the show! Our participation, encouragement, and support make Disney World a success. It's reflected in the memories we take away from our visit there.

My grandmother, Jessie! I remember a time when she was 83 years old and in the hospital. One night, waking up a bit disoriented, she got out of bed, grabbed her intravenous fluid stand, still wearing her nightgown, started down the hall toward the hospital's main entrance. It was 2 a.m. and a cold winter in Chicago.

Harold, a janitor working the graveyard shift, saw

her leaving and acted quickly. He gently blocked her way, read her hospital identification tag and said, "Jessie, what in the world are you doing out here? It's cold outside. Let me get you back to your room."

I heard about the incident later that morning and asked the head nurse, "How did the janitor know to do this instead of just continuing to do his janitorial chores?"

Amazed by my question, she replied, "Mr. Dawson, everyone in this hospital takes part in providing health care service."

Indeed, everyone does have a role in the show and the same is true for a community. We must all be involved in raising our kids.

Eight
Mr. Dawson Goes to Washington

IT was 5:30 a.m. when Robert Dawson awoke in his Washington, D.C. townhouse. It was Friday and he had to be at the U.S. Department of Education headquarters by 7:30 a.m.

He completed his morning routine in half the time. He caught the metro subway into the district and arrived at his office a full half-hour before the meeting with the Secretary of Education was to begin.

He looked over his notes. He realized the Secretary called this emergency meeting to discuss a policy crisis. Still, Robert asked the Secretary's chief of staff to allow him 15 minutes in front of the Secretary to discuss issues that he felt were enormously important. His request was approved. However, he was granted only 10 minutes to speak.

"Packed agenda," was the chief of staff's explanation.

It was almost 7:30 a.m. and Robert hurried down the hall to take his seat in the Secretary's conference room.

Most of his colleagues had arrived early and at exactly 7:30 a.m., the Secretary of Education arrived.

"Thank you all for joining me this morning," the Secretary began. "I understand some of you had to cut short your out-of-town trips and postpone meetings. I apologize for the inconvenience, but I felt it important to call the senior staff together to address a major policy issue which the President has asked us to review and formulate opinions on. The President plans to address these issues and our findings at his press conference Monday morning."

The Secretary continued, "Four days ago, the President's Commission on the Future of America's Children released its report. The report raised a number of issues about our children and their futures. The report's three major findings included:"

1. America's children have great difficulty relating their educational experiences to real-world values. Too many students are not connecting what our schools are teaching to what they need to succeed as adults.

2. America's children do not believe their futures to be bright.

3. America's children believe that adults are detached from children's lives and therefore, children only get token support when support is needed.

The Secretary then showed his audience newspapers from across the country.

"After the release of the study, every major news service and newspaper ran stories with these headlines," the Secretary said.

- **"FUTURES BLEAK FOR YOUTH"**
- **"CHILDREN LACK HOPE"**
- **"WHERE HAVE ALL THE ADULTS GONE?"**
- **"HOPELESSNESS MAJOR CONCERN FOR AMERICA'S YOUTH"**

"So, ladies and gentlemen, our task is to offer the President some options, to address what he and I believe to be, a crisis of 'hope.' In a personal call to me, the President said he was very concerned," the Secretary said.

"The President told me that 'America is the country that was built on hope. America's youth are its flame. America's youth are our future. If they don't see a bright future for themselves, then America doesn't have a bright future. It's as simple as that,'" he continued.

"I'm open to suggestions," concluded the Secretary.

It was hard for Robert not to spring to his feet. He'd just spent so much time learning about hope. Now, he faced the Secretary of Education who was asking for suggestions about what to do with a crisis concerning America's youth. Although Robert requested 15-minutes on the agenda to discuss a topic, he didn't know where to start.

"Mr. Secretary," Robert spoke.

"Yes, Robert. Please, what insights to you have?" the Secretary asked.

"Sir, I spent the past few days visiting a school which was identified as offering exemplary programs. I left my visit with a greater understanding that America's future and the solutions to its problems do not lie with another well-meaning program, but rather, are rooted in the same foundation that has existed since 1776. That foundation, Mr. Secretary, is our country's belief that all its children can be successful, and there are no exceptions!" explained Robert excitedly.

"Mr. Secretary," Robert continued, "let me share with you a most remarkable experience, with the guarantee that the President and all Americans have little to be concerned with, if we can effectively challenge our nation to see its children more positively and encourage everyone to support our children's futures."

"Go on, Mr. Dawson," requested the Secretary.

"Well, it starts with,'You gotta believe!' Let me elaborate..."

Conclusion: From Parable to Reality, The Kids at Hope Story Continues

Don't be fooled into believing that our story is too naïve to possibly be true. The fact is, this story reflects the successes of the many groups, organizations, institutions, and agencies across the country which have adopted the Kids at Hope belief system and strategy in support of the success of all children. These courageous organizations have come to understand that it isn't a program which makes a difference in a child's life it is first and foremost our belief in them, followed by a meaningful relationship with caring adults and finally the understanding of the importance of focusing on their futures. Only then, can the programs we provide ever make a difference.

Contact Kids at Hope at www.kidsathope.org to learn more about the communities and groups across the country, which are modeling the examples offered in this book.

Kids at Hope provides professional staff and volunteer development, consulting, and coaching, program enhancements. Research and evaluation are available to support the goals and objectives associated with creating a culture where all children can succeed without exception.

Please contact us if you share our belief that our children are at hope rather than at risk; and wish to learn more or join the thousands of individuals and groups in this powerful initiative.

Kids at Hope Believed and Practiced Here
www.kidsathope.org

John P. Carlos

Born August 4, 1943 • Died April 25, 2004

Hundreds of audiences have come away from John's presentations uttering their praise. "An amazing storyteller!" His poignant, humorous, powerful, and practical "storytelling" style has wowed audiences around the world. Combining his business experience in the private and public sector, his stories were rich with human condition and powerful with applications that affected his clients' personal and professional lives.

John had the ability to draw you into his stories with humor and common sense. His talent for causing people to examine their own behavior first is a magnificent methodology for effecting change in organizational and personal lives. He had a unique ability to make people laugh while they learned.

John co-authored his first book with Ken Blanchard and Alan Randolph. *Empowerment Takes More Than A Minute,* immediately climbed to #7 on *Business Week's* best-seller list. It has since gone on to sell over 400,000 copies in less than two years and is translated into 19 languages. This was followed by the equally successful, *Three Keys to Empowerment.*

John Carlos was a senior consulting partner with The Ken Blanchard Companies, a full-service management training and consulting company with global headquarters in San Diego, California. His past experiences include director of training for the Circle K Corporation,

14 years as the executive director of various Boys and Girls Club of America member agencies and several years running his own school, Celebration.

He was voted one of the Outstanding Young Men in America by the United States Chamber of Commerce and is a Vietnam-era veteran of the U.S. Army. John was a member of American Society of Training and Development, a member of the faculty of the American College of Physician Executives, and a graduate of the San Bernardino County Sheriff's Academy. He was awarded the "Key to the City of Indio, California" for outstanding community service and is a past president of the Running Springs Area Chamber of Commerce.

John received his bachelor's degree in business and a masters degree in business administration from Columbia Pacific University. John was a Life Member of the American Camping Association. He is survived by his wife of 35 years Lynne, and has two daughters and four granddaughters.

Rick Miller

From the school house to the clubhouse and then on to the White House, Rick Miller has spent 40 years advocating, teaching, and supporting all America's children and youth.

In 1981 Rick served in The White House as a loaned executive in support of the President's Task Force on Private Sector Initiatives. Rick has also testified before congress on a number of issues affecting youth and the not for profit sector.

For 30 years Rick was an executive with the Boys & Girls Clubs of America, including serving as the National Director for Government Relations.

In 1998 Rick was appointed Arizona State University's first Practitioner in Residence serving the Center for Leadership and Non Profit Management.

Rick founded Kids at Hope in 1999, a national initiative designed to change the paradigm from youth at risk to Kids at Hope. Currently, Kids at Hope has trained over 14,000 caring adults, and is supporting 350 organizations across the country reaching over 300,000 children.

Rick has published a number of influential articles on fund raising, organizational development, and youth services. Additionally, he has written two books, *From Youth at Risk to Kids at Hope: A journey into the belief system where all children are capable of success, No Exceptions!* and *Kids at Hope: Every Child Can Succeed, No Exceptions,* co-authored by international best-selling author John Carlos and foreword by Dr. Ken Blanchard of *The One Minute Manager* fame.

In addition to his Kids at Hope duties, Rick is on the faculty at Arizona State University.

Rick's breadth of understanding about youth development from a research, academic, and practitioners perspective establishes his credentials as one of America's most informed and effective spokespersons for children. Rick is able to translate and bridge complicated theory into straightforward and powerful expressions about what is best for youth.

Rick crosses over all disciplines and is highly sought as a keynote speaker and presenter to academic, recreation, education, youth development, and law enforcement audiences all over the country. His wit, humor, and story telling abilities captivate the imagination of his audiences leaving everyone who hears him believing that all children are truly capable of success. *NO EXCEPTIONS!*

Rick is a husband, father, and grandfather. He lives in Phoenix, Arizona.